Survival Guide
for
College Students
with
ADD or LD

Survival Guide
for
College Students
with
ADD or LD

Kathleen G. Nadeau, Ph.D.

Magination Press ● New York

Library of Congress Cataloging-in-Publication Data

Nadeau, Kathleen G.
    Survival guide for college students with ADD or LD / by
Kathleen G. Nadeau.
        p.   cm.
    Includes bibliographical references.
    ISBN 0-945354-63-0
    1. Learning disabled–Education (Higher)–United States.
2. Attention-deficit-disordered youth–Education (Higher)–
United States. I. Title.
LC4818.5.N33 1994
371.9–dc20   94-15724
                                          CIP

Published by
MAGINATION PRESS
an Imprint of Brunner/Mazel, Inc.
19 Union Square West
New York, NY 10003
(800) 825-3089

Manufactured in the United States of America

10 9 8 7 6 5 4 3

Acknowledgments

I want to express my thanks and appreciation to Christy Willis, Director of Disabled Student Services at The George Washington University, to Joy Cobb, the student liaison of the LD Resource Group at George Washington University, and to all the members of the LD Resource Group for their cooperation, patience and support. Christy's presence on campus and her involvement and genuine caring for the students who seek her help is a major factor in why so many students with ADD/LD find success on the GWU campus. All of the students photographed for this book are diagnosed with ADD or LD. They generously made their time available, and allowed us into their meetings and classes for a glimpse into the life of a college student with ADD/LD.

Thanks (and hugs) also go to my daughter, Langdon Nadeau, a college student with learning and attention problems, for her insights and input into this book, and especially for her suggestion that we add photographs of students to the book. Thanks also to Mary Richard, a member of the CH.A.D.D. National Board of Directors, and a staff member of the Disability Support Services office at the University of Iowa, for her very helpful review and comments.

I cannot express enough appreciation to our photographer, Sylvia Johnson, a professional photographer with an interest in ADD/LD issues, for her tireless patience. She went above and beyond the call of duty in her repeated forays onto campus to accommodate the complicated and changing schedules of the students while she photographed the pictures for this book.

Without all of their help this project would not have been possible.

TABLE OF CONTENTS

INTRODUCTION

This book has been written for college students with attention deficit disorder (ADD) or learning disabilities (LD) who are applying to college, or who may already be enrolled in college.

Note: *We use the term ADD throughout this book as a comprehensive term to include both hyperactive and nonhyperactive students with attention deficit disorder. Generally, we use the term ADD/LD, and only use ADD or LD separately when the topic clearly applies to only one or the other.*

Many colleges and universities are becoming more aware of the needs of students with learning and attention problems. New programs are developed every year as colleges and universities begin to evaluate their programs with your needs in mind. There has never been a better time for students with ADD/LD to be attending college. You should be aware, however, that not all colleges are equally prepared to serve you. In this book we will talk about how to evaluate the colleges to which you apply, or the school you currently attend, to determine whether it can provide the service and support you need.

Few colleges yet have specific ADD services. ADD is such a new concept on the college campus that only a tiny handful of colleges have ADD specialists. Don't despair though. Most of the services and supports that are appropriate for students with LD are appropriate for students with ADD as well. Also, services that are not provided on campus may be available in the community in which your college is based.

Success in college for students with learning and attention problems requires a working partnership between you and the people providing services at your college. You need to be informed about your learning style and specific problem areas that require accommodations. This book is designed to help you gain the information you need to be an effective self-advocate.

The following pages are filled with tips and advice gathered from college students like yourself, and from specialists in the fields of learning disabilities and attention deficit disorder, about how to survive and succeed in the college setting.

SECTION 1

CHOOSING A COLLEGE

Making the Decision

How do you choose a college that is right for you? Maybe
you have talked to your friends and want to apply to
schools they know about. Maybe you plan to go to the
nearest state university, a competitive liberal arts college or
a "Big 10" school. Whatever your dreams or plans may be,
in order to make a good choice you will need to consider
your problems with learning and concentration.

Many high school students try to ignore their ADD or LD
problems when they select a college. In high school, the LD
label may have felt like a liability, a label to shed in a new
environment. If this is your attitude, you should still
consider applying to schools with good ADD/LD programs.
Even if you do not plan to use the ADD/LD services, you
will be at a great advantage by attending a school where
such services are available. Later, if you find that you are
experiencing academic difficulties, the services will be there
waiting for you.

A faculty fully aware of the needs of ADD/LD students will
benefit you directly, whether or not you use the "label"
because such a faculty is attuned to students with different
learning styles and needs, and has been taught to be more
flexible in requirements and teaching style. Often such
teachers will identify students in their classes as possible
ADD or LD and will refer them for testing.

Before you make a final decision about whether to take
advantage of services for students with learning or attention difficulties, you should be aware that the social stigma
you may have experienced in grade school or high school is
not an issue on the college campus. You will not be rel-
egated to a "dummy class" or be embarrassed in any way.
In schools with supportive attitudes and programs, you will

simply find yourself receiving the services you need to be successful.

As a general rule, in selecting a college look for schools with small classes and a well-developed, high quality ADD/LD support program.

Assessing Services

Students with learning disabilities and attention problems need to carefully assess the Office of Disabled Student Services on each campus they are considering. This office should be very active in advocating for students with learning problems. How do you find this out? Here are some questions you should ask the director of the DSS office:

- Is the director of the Office of Disabled Student Services a specialist in attention deficit disorder and learning disabilities?

- How many students with ADD or LD are registered with the DSS office?

- How long has the support program for students with ADD/LD existed?

- Is there a formal LD program for students on campus? Does a student have to make separate application to this program?

- Are there extra charges for the program?

- Is there an ADD specialist or special services for ADD students?

- Is there a faculty education program to familiarize the faculty with needs of students with ADD or LD?

- What kinds of accommodations does this school offer students with special needs?

- Is specialized tutoring available for students with LD?

- Are there any ADD/LD support groups on campus?

- Are there seminars or courses for students with ADD and LD that teach study skills or self-advocacy skills?

- How complicated is the procedure a student must follow to obtain alternative testing (extended time or taking a written test on a computer)?

- Is there a specialist on campus who teaches planning, organizational, and study skills?

- Do students with ADD and LD have early registration privileges to allow them to select the courses and professors they need?

- Does the school offer specialized academic advising through the DSS office for students with ADD and LD?

- Does the school help students identify faculty members who are knowledgeable about and sympathetic toward ADD and LD issues?

- What is the attitude of the school toward accommodating a student who is unable to pass a math or foreign language requirement? Are requirements ever waived? Are course substitutions allowed?

- Are students required to fail language or math courses before they can qualify for a foreign language waiver?

- Are students who receive services for ADD/LD through the DSS office available for applicants to talk to?

- Are counselors available on an ongoing basis for ADD/LD counseling and support?

After asking these questions you will be a much better judge of how well each school can meet your particular needs.

Avoiding Pitfalls

You may feel that you have already learned to compensate for your learning problems and do not need ADD/LD services in college. While this may be generally true, a thoughtful college selection can sometimes make the difference between graduation and failure to complete your degree. Ignoring learning problems in the beginning may lead to trouble further down the road. Some of the most common stumbling blocks that can keep a bright, capable student with ADD or LD from graduating are:

◆ **Math requirements.**
If math is an area of weakness for you, you should carefully investigate the math requirement of the schools to

which you apply. A few schools have no general math requirement. Other schools are flexible about course waivers or have only a minimal math requirement.

◆ Foreign language requirements.
If foreign languages are difficult for you, you should carefully examine each school's policy regarding foreign languages. Some schools are more flexible than others. If you are unable to pass two or more years of foreign language, explore whether the school will allow substitution of a foreign culture course, or a foreign literature course taught in translation. Another possibility is to substitute a sign language course for a foreign language course.

You may find it easier to fulfill your language requirement by participating in a language immersion program for a summer or a semester.

◆ Discouragement and low grades.
A failure and discouragement cycle can be set in motion if you attend a school that does not have a good ADD/LD support program and an informed faculty. Many students with ADD or LD have failed or dropped out of such schools. Later they may transfer to schools where they succeed due to better support services and more supportive teachers.

You may also enter into a failure cycle because you do not involve yourself in the ADD/LD support program and do not learn to use the available accommodations.

◆ Senior thesis or project.
A senior thesis or project may become your ultimate stumbling block even though you have otherwise been able to complete all undergraduate requirements. Not all schools require a senior thesis or senior project; however, many of the highly competitive schools do have such a requirement. Certain courses of study may require senior projects. If long-term planning and follow-through are significant problems for you, don't take the risk of selecting a school or a major that requires a long-term senior project.

SECTION 2

HELP ON CAMPUS

Accommodations and Strategies

The following is a list of strategies (to be employed by the student) and accommodations (to be provided by the school) for students with ADD/LD. Effort is needed on both sides for your success. A later section will focus more on the student side of the success equation.

Every student should be aware of his or her legal rights. Asking for accommodations is not asking for a "favor." It is simply availing yourself of legally mandated assistance. Students' rights are protected under the Rehabilitation Act (RA) of 1973 and the Americans with Disabilities Act (ADA), which bar discrimination, and by the Individuals with Disabilities Education Act (IDEA), which mandates free, appropriate education at the primary and secondary levels. Combining the RA with the IDEA extends this mandate to the college level.

Schools are not required by law to change their admission standards or requirements for graduation, but they are required to provide accommodations for your ADD or learning disabilities. Do not feel apologetic about requesting accommodations, and do not wait until you are in academic trouble. It is your responsibility to ask for help, and it is the school's responsibility to provide that help.

◆ **General accommodations and strategies.**
Arrange to have your exam schedule altered so that you don't have more than one final exam or mid-term per day.

Arrange for proctored, extended-time examinations through your professor or through the DSS office.

Choose classes that offer small discussion groups rather than a lecture format whenever possible.

Ask your counselor at the DSS office to help you compose a brief, succinct description of your attention and/or learning problems and the types of accommodations and assistance you will require from your professors. Have copies of this statement printed on DSS office stationery to present, as an official statement, to each of your professors.

Arrange through the DSS office to have a note-taker in each class that is difficult for you. In many schools this note-taking arrangement can be done anonymously so that you won't feel self-conscious or embarrassed.

Write each professor's office hours down in a single, organized list. Use those office hours regularly. Make sure your professor knows who you are and what accommodations you need.

◆ Problems with writing.
Arrange for easy, frequent access to a word processor. With use of a spell-checker and grammar checker, proofing can be done directly on the computer, eliminating the possibility of reintroducing errors onto your final copy.

Explain your written language disability to your professors and request that they not discount your grade for spelling and punctuation errors on in-class writing assignments.

If you have severe writing problems, request oral examinations.

Have a peer or tutor routinely review all writing assignments before preparing a final draft.

Use a lap top computer for taking notes in class and in the library.

Make frequent use of support available at the campus writing center when preparing written assignments.

◆ Word retrieval and memory problems.
Go to your professor early in the term to explain your memory difficulties. Make a request for accommodations

before you experience difficulty in the class. A professor who is convinced that you are diligent and motivated will be much more likely to modify exams or to allow extra-credit work.

Request of your professor that you not be examined using fill-in-the-blank or other brief-answer questions. Multiple-choice or essay exam questions will allow you to demonstrate what you *do* know rather than what you can't recall.

Request more frequent quizzes and take home exams if you tend to do poorly in classes that have only heavily weighted midterms and finals.

Work with a tutor to learn how to develop memory skills. With the tutor's help, assess whether you are a better visual or auditory learner. Plan your study techniques accordingly.

Learn to quiz yourself prior to exams. Many students mistake recognition memory for retrieval memory. That is, some students mistakenly assume that when information seems familiar, they "know" it. Recognizing and understanding material that is presented to you is not equivalent to being able to retrieve, organize, and explain that same material.

◆ Attention problems.

Tape record lectures or have access to a complete set of lecture notes provided either by the professor or by a fellow student. (This is also useful for students who have auditory processing difficulties or are unable to write quickly enough to take good notes.)

Sign up for small classes for better concentration and fewer distractions.

Sit away from a window or door that may be distracting.

Actively participate in class discussions to increase your concentration.

◆ Reading difficulty.

Have your texts and reading assignments recorded. Your DSS office may offer this service free of charge. This service requires that you plan in advance. As a general rule, allow at least four to six weeks.

Avoid multiple-choice exams. Inform your professor that your reading comprehension difficulties make it hard to accurately comprehend and correctly answer multiple-choice questions. Request questions that require a short answer instead.

If your reading comprehension difficulties lead you to be unsure about the meaning of an exam question, don't hesitate to ask the professor to rephrase the question. (This request will receive a more accommodating response if you have informed the professor of your reading comprehension difficulties prior to the exam.)

Form study groups. In a study group you can check your understanding of reading material through discussion with other students.

Academic Counseling

Specific academic counseling can help guide you to maximize your strengths and minimize your weaknesses. Counseling should be done by an ADD/LD specialist in the campus DSS office who has an intimate knowledge of your areas of disability. You should make sure that the school you select provides this type of specialized counseling. Too many ADD/LD students have an academic advisor who is a busy faculty member with little time and no expertise in advising students with special needs.

Your counselor should help guide you toward professors who are knowledgeable and supportive of students with ADD or LD. Ideally, your DSS office should develop a list of student-recommended professors who are best for students with ADD or LD.

Academic counseling should help you develop a well-thought-out class schedule each term.

A good support program should allow students with ADD or LD early registration each term so that you can be sure to have access to the courses and professors that you need.

Scheduling Classes

Don't sign up for several courses with heavy reading or writing requirements during the same term.

If possible, avoid successive classes without a break.

Avoid classes that meet for longer than one hour. In longer classes, your concentration will wane and so will your ability to learn.

Try to mix your most interesting classes with required courses that may interest you less.

Make sure that your schedule is balanced each term by not including many classes that tax your areas of disability.

Be realistic. If you are a night owl who has great difficulty getting up in the morning, look for a class schedule that doesn't begin earlier than 10:00 a.m. If you will be leaving campus frequently on weekends, don't sign up for a class that meets late on Friday. Signing up for a class you will likely miss will greatly reduce your chances for success.

Take a reduced course load of 12 semester hours. Most students with ADD or LD function much better by taking fewer courses.

Course Selection and Registration

Take full advantage of early registration privileges — an accommodation available to ADD/LD students at many schools. Invest time in talking to other students and to your DSS office to learn which are the best teachers and courses.

Students with ADD or LD should make full use of the "drop and add" period. (This is the first week or two of classes each term in which you are allowed to change your schedule.) If after the first few classes, you feel that your professor is inflexible, unwilling to give you the accommodations you need, or teaches in a style that cannot hold your attention, drop the class and arrange for an alternate selection.

Talk to your professors about their knowledge of ADD and LD. Select the ones who seem informed and supportive.

Carefully review the syllabus of each course after the first class. Evaluate whether the reading and writing assignments are possible for you to fulfill given your other course work. Avoid large lectures if at all possible. Small classes with group discussion will enhance your comprehension and concentration.

Register for more classes than you plan to take. This allows you to drop some of your classes without having to change the rest of your schedule.

Selecting a Major

Most college students enter college with little notion of what they want to study. Sometimes students approaching the end of their sophomore year choose their major almost randomly. "Let's see, I already have three history courses. Maybe I'll major in history." Other students base the choice on the inspiration of a favorite professor. It is not unusual for students to change their selection of a major at least once.

The selection of a major is a more critical choice for ADD/ LD students than for the typical college student. It is essential that you make a choice that will emphasize your strengths and minimize your areas of weakness.

In order to make a good choice, it can be helpful to list your strengths. Many students with ADD/LD are more aware of their learning weaknesses than of their strengths. Don't limit yourself to purely academic strengths. Such a list of strengths might include:

Good with people	Verbal expression
Love to talk	Writing
Lots of energy	Reading
Determination	Good reasoning ability
Good problem-solver	Artistic
Lots of ideas	

Then write a list of areas of difficulty. These might include:

Tend to overlook details	Science
Dislike paperwork	Math
Absent-minded	Memory problems

Go over these lists with your advisor to receive assistance in making a good match between your strengths, weaknesses, and the academic requirements in each major. You should also consider probable job requirements after college, as well as whether you will need graduate training in your chosen field. Don't let your areas of weakness completely dictate your choice, however. If you have a burning desire to study a particular subject, by all means pursue that interest. Your extra motivation can help you overcome the obstacles presented by your learning problems.

Career Guidance

Specialized career counseling is particularly important for the ADD or LD student. Such counseling ideally should involve *ability* testing in addition to *disability* testing to assess learning problems. Personality testing and interest testing are also important. All of this information combined enables a career counselor to engage in a fruitful dialogue with you about optimal career directions. Don't expect to be given one or two specific career choices. A good career counselor will talk to you about general areas of ability and interest, and will help guide you toward a choice within these areas.

◆ **Interest inventories.**
Look at your interests in relation to your strengths and weaknesses. Interest inventories, available through your college counseling center, can provide useful information. They can help you think in a more organized manner about your clusters of interests and the types of jobs that utilize such interests.

◆ **Personality testing.**
You may want to take the Myers-Briggs Type Inventory at your college counseling center. This is a personality inventory that will place you in a particular "personality type." Many studies have been done about which personality types tend to function well in particular professions. Your MBTI results provide important information assisting you in choosing a college major.

◆ **Ability testing.**
There are a number of ability tests available today. Some of these are offered privately; others are offered through the

Department of Rehabilitative Services. Many students with ADD or LD become overly focused on their disability, and may ignore or be unaware of special abilities. A good ability test battery will analyze clusters of natural ability and can direct you toward career paths that will maximize their use. All of these various types of testing can provide you with valuable information to help you make your career decision.

Make your decision a positive choice rather than an avoidance of negative choices. All too many students with ADD/LD approach the selection of their major from a negative standpoint. "Let's see. I'm not good in math, so I shouldn't take science courses." Or, "I'm a slow reader, so I shouldn't take anything in the humanities." Students who make their choices through a process of elimination may find themselves in a field that doesn't really interest them.

It is much better to take a positive, problem-solving approach. For example: "What I'd really like to do is go into business. I know that I have difficulty with math, and that math is required to earn a business degree. Let me talk to my advisor and to someone in the business school to explore my options. Maybe some course substitutions would be allowed. Perhaps there are some areas of business that emphasize math less than others."

The key to a positive career choice is to follow your heart's desire while being realistic about your strengths and weaknesses.

◆ **Tutoring.**
At many colleges tutoring is available free of charge as an accommodation for ADD and LD students through the federally funded TRIO program. Other colleges provide specialized tutoring for a fee. You should inquire through your DSS office what services are available at your school.

SECTION 3

HELP IN THE COMMUNITY

Medical Consultation

You may need to supplement the services available on campus by seeking professionals in the community who specialize in working with college students who have attention and/or learning difficulties.

If you have been diagnosed with ADD and prescribed medication by a physician at home, you may need to obtain a referral to a physician in your college community who can provide continuing care. Few physicians have experience in treating college students with ADD, but it is important that you find a doctor with expertise and experience. This professional may be associated with student health services on campus, with a university medical center, or may be a psychiatrist or neurologist in the community.

You will need to get copies of all your evaluation and treatment records from home in order to facilitate a smooth transition to ADD treatment with a new doctor. If your physician at home cannot refer you to someone at your college or in your college community, a good way to obtain names of qualified physicians is to contact the local CH.A.D.D. (Children and Adults with Attention Deficit Disorder) chapter in your college community. You can obtain the name and phone number of the local representative by calling CH.A.D.D. headquarters (see the Resources listing at the back of this book).

Follow-up care is essential to good treatment for ADD. Obtaining prescriptions for Ritalin or Dexedrine can be complicated. Because they are controlled substances, these prescriptions cannot be phoned to a pharmacy, and out-of-state prescriptions will not be honored. For these reasons, you should find a physician in your college town who can work with you.

Counseling or Psychotherapy

Many students with learning and attention difficulties have developed problems with self-esteem, with interpersonal relationships, or with anxiety and depression. Such difficulties should not be ignored. To succeed in college, you will need to focus your energy on academic pursuits. If you are struggling with emotional troubles, self-doubts, loneliness, or social isolation, your academic tasks may become insurmountable. Don't wait until you are in a crisis state before seeking help. If your college counseling services offers only short-term help, ask for a referral to a mental health professional in the community who has experience working with students who have learning and/or attention difficulties.

You may need support, advice, and counseling as you make the transition to independent college living. A complete treatment program for ADD involves not only medication, but also counseling to learn to make realistic decisions, to understand your ADD better, and to learn mechanisms to cope with the stress and frustration that often accompany ADD. Although you may decide to try it on your own for a while, it is a good idea to have the names of a couple of professionals on campus or in your college community who you can contact if the need arises.

Specialized Tutoring

Many students in college need a more specialized type of tutoring than may be offered on campus. If you cannot find a tutor trained in working with ADD/LD students on campus, it may well be worth the added expense to seek such tutoring privately. This support is particularly important as you make the transition from high school to college. Tutoring should focus on study, planning, and organizational skills as well as specific areas of difficulty. If your learning disabilities involve both reading or written language and math you may need different tutors for each area. If your campus DSS office cannot refer you to a good tutor, you may be able to obtain a list of names through the

local Learning Disability Association (LDA) or through the
local CH.A.D.D. chapter.

SECTION 4

HELPING YOURSELF

Study Tips

Accept that you will have to study longer and harder than some other students.

Study in a distraction-free environment — alone in your dorm room, or in the library. Some students find the library distracting. Studying in the library stacks or in an empty classroom may help. Some schools set aside quiet areas for study at night.

If long-term concentration is difficult, study in one-hour segments. Do not set aside long periods of time to complete writing assignments or study for an exam. You will probably find that you do not make efficient use of this time.

Develop a regular study routine. The more you stick to it the easier it will be.

If you learn best auditorily, read aloud to yourself while studying.

Another tip for auditory learners is to form a study group for most of your classes. These groups can discuss class notes and study for tests by quizzing each other.

When studying alone, take notes by dictating into a hand-held tape recorder. Your learning and concentration will be greatly enhanced by briefly summarizing paragraphs or key points while you read.

Learn as much as you can about your best learning style. Are you an auditory learner, a visual learner, or a hands-on learner? Work with your tutor to maximize using your best style.

Consciously study memory techniques. There are a number of books available on the subject that can help you learn to enhance your memory.

Learn to "overlearn." Students with memory problems need more practice trials. After you seem to know all the material, to be sure you have it in long-term storage, you will need to develop "overlearning" strategies. Learn the material "backwards and forwards." For example, study from the word to the definition, then later go from the definition to naming the word. Try to explain the material to someone who knows nothing about it. See if you can answer their questions. Teaching someone else is an excellent way of learning for yourself.

Be an active learner.

- Skim the chapter to learn what it is generally about.

- Turn chapter headings into questions. This will give you a focus when you read the chapter.

- After formulating your questions, read the text to locate the answers.

- Recite the answer to your question, then paraphrase it aloud.

- After paraphrasing the answer to each question in the chapter, briefly review the major points, reading each heading aloud and attempting to recall points of information under it. Return to the material at a later time for a second review.

This study technique is an active learning technique. Many students study passively. They may simply start at the beginning and read through the chapter, hoping to recall what they have read. They may highlight key words or phrases, but do little else to actively learn the material. An active learner, however, constantly works with the material asking, "What does this remind me of? What can I associate this with in order to remember? How can I say this in my own words? What is the main point?"

Sit in the front and middle of each class whenever possible. These are the "success seats," which keep you attending, and show your professor that you have come to learn.

Develop a working relationship with each of your professors. Make sure they know you and what your needs are.

Auditory learners will benefit from tape recording each class. Listening to tapes may be more useful than repeatedly reading written material.

Have a peer or tutor routinely review all writing assignments before preparing a final draft.

Use a lap top computer for in-class note-taking, and for taking notes in the library.

Learn to actively quiz yourself prior to exams.

Time Management

Managing time is a major problem for many students with ADD or LD. You may need to devote much more time to studying than the average student. Having more time available requires better time management skills.

Make a habit of a 10 to 15 minute daily planning period to map out your day.

Don't overbook yourself. If you need extra time to study, you may need to take a reduced course load or eliminate some of your extracurricular activities.

Develop the habit of using your between-class hours for study. Although it is tempting to go to the snack bar for a coke or head back to the dorm for a break, you will find that you are more effective studying in hour-long segments throughout the day rather than studying for several hours at night.

Think proactively rather than reactively. Stick to your plan and keep control of your use of time rather than reacting to the impulse of the moment, or by responding to the request of some other person.

Planning

In college you have more unstructured time than you had in high school and more than you will probably have after you enter the professional world. Many students, unaccustomed to so much "free" time, don't plan their reading assignments and their long-term projects. As a student with ADD/LD, you probably aren't able to work as efficiently as other students. Some students with ADD/LD have college transcripts liberally scattered with course withdrawals after they discover at midterm they are too far behind to catch up on postponed reading or writing assignments. You need to realize from the outset that you cannot rely on a last minute approach and must plan your time from the beginning of each term.

◆ Using day planners.

A day planner is a calendar with a page devoted to each day of the year. In high school, your day is essentially planned for you. You need only to write down your assignments. In college, most of the hours of each day are unstructured. Using a day planner will help you structure your days to make sure you are keeping up with the work you need to do.

During the first week of classes, each professor should supply you with a course syllabus, which outlines reading, writing, and lab assignments. Take the syllabus from each course and record the dates of all exams and the due dates for reading and writing assignments in your day planner.

For each reading assignment, divide it into small "bites." Be realistic. If you are a slow reader and tend to lose concentration while reading, don't expect to read an entire chapter in economics at one sitting. The more "dense" the reading material (that is, the more detailed new information is in the assignment), the more time you need to devote to it. For example, you might be able to read 75 pages of a novel assigned for an English class at one sitting, but you may only be able to concentrate on 10 pages of your chemistry text before you need a break.

If you are assigned to read two chapters in chemistry during the first two weeks of class, look at your text and estimate how many pages you can read with good concentration at one sitting. If you estimate 10 pages and the two chapters are 45 pages, you need to assign five reading periods for your chemistry class. Take your day planner and block out five one-hour time segments over the two-week period.

All activities and commitments should be written in your day planner, with the times blocked out. On the next page is an example of how a typical day in a college student's day planner might look.

✓	TO DO:		SCHEDULE:
		:30	
✓	LAUNDRY	8:00	Breakfast
		:30	
✓	LIBRARY –	9:00	Start Laundry
	get references	:30	
	for paper	10:00	Chemistry
		:30	
	Pay parking	11:00	Library
	ticket!	:30	
		12:00	Lunch
✓	Call Lisa	:30	
		1:00	Anthropology
	make appt	:30	
	with	2:00	Errands
	tutor	:30	
		3:00	Chemistry Lab
		:30	
		4:00	↓
		:30	
	couldn't reach	5:00	/// BREAK ////
	him – call	:30	
	tomorrow	6:00	Dinner Put Laundry in dryer
		:30	
		7:00	Study
		:30	
		8:00	
		:30	Read Anthro. Ch. 3
		9:00	↓
		:30	
		10:00	/// BREAK ////
		:30	Read
		11:00	Write tomorrow's schedule
		:30	
		12:00	Bedtime Turn off TV!

◆ Planning long-term projects.

If you have a 25-page paper to write, break the large project into a list of smaller tasks. These task might be:

1. Discuss possible topics with professor.
2. Go to library and do a "literature search" on your selected topic. Copy the list of references.
3. Go to library and make copies of relevant articles.
4. Read, underline, and outline five articles on large note cards.
5. Read, underline, and outline five more articles.
6. Read, underline, and outline the remaining articles.
7. Make a list of relevant books and authors. Be sure to copy all information needed for your bibliography.
8. Take notes from the books you have selected for your paper. (Talk to your tutor about how to glean needed information from a book without having to read the entire book.)
9. Make an initial outline for your paper. Discuss the outline with your professor.

10. Write a rough draft of the paper on a computer. Use spell check and grammar check.
11. Type your bibliography on the computer.
12. Take your rough draft to your tutor. Work on the organization and structure of your paper. Get help on ways to develop and elaborate your ideas.
13. Write the final draft of your paper.
14. Take the final draft to your tutor for assistance with final revisions.
15. Make revisions on the computer and print your final copy.

After you have made a task list such as the one above, estimate how much time you will need for each task. Write the estimated time next to each task. Then go to your day planner and assign a day and time for each task. One way to do this is to begin with the date the paper is due and work backward. Some students find that a large, monthly calendar is useful for charting a lengthy project.

Overcoming Procrastination

Procrastination is often one of the biggest enemies of accomplishment. We may procrastinate for several reasons. Lets look at some possible reasons and ways to combat them.

◆ Lack of motivation.
Many students put off assignments in classes that don't interest them. Students with ADD or LD often have such a problem. It is essential that you select a major that excites you and that is compatible with your strengths and weaknesses. (Refer back to the section Selecting a Major.)

◆ Learn to motivate yourself.
Even with the selection of an appropriate major, there will be required courses that hold little interest for you. You need to find ways to motivate yourself to work in these courses. One good way is to use the activities you *want to do* as rewards for doing those activities you *ought to do*. Use lots of little rewards for a particularly unpleasant or difficult task. Some possible motivators are:

Going to get a soft drink or snack.
Making a phone call.
Visiting with a friend or roommate.
Taking a walk.
Watching a little TV.

Be sure to give yourself a time limit because these short breaks can easily turn into long ones. If you find that a 15-minute break often turns into a 60-minute break, set a timer for yourself and then get back to work.

Schedule bigger rewards at the end of your day. For example, "If I get all the way through *all* of the planned activities in my day planner, I'll go out with my friends to a movie tonight."

Even larger rewards can be scheduled for bigger accomplishments. "When I finish my political science term paper, I'll go away for the weekend."

◆ Fear of failure.

Many students with ADD or LD feel overwhelmed by courses or assignments. They put off beginning a project because they doubt they are capable of completing it. Some ways of combating this are:

- Ask for feedback from your tutor or DSS counselor to assess whether your fear is realistic.

- Don't keep putting it off. The longer you put it off, the bigger it will look as the deadlines draw ever nearer.

- Talk to your professor. Tell him or her that you need help.

- Go to your tutor and ask for help on the project.

◆ Not knowing how to begin.

Don't be afraid to ask. Many students fear they will appear to be "dumb" if they tell their professor they don't know how to get started. Talk to your professor to be sure you understand all of the requirements and expectations for the project. Then go to your tutor and ask for help in planning the project.

◆ When the task looks bigger than you are.

Divide and conquer. Break the task down into as many small pieces as you can think of. Write each task down as a "to do" item in your day planner. Give yourself a check mark each time you finish a small task. Seeing all the check marks can give you a sense of accomplishment.

Don't look at the top of the hill. As you begin your "ascent" of the big project, don't look at everything you will have to do. Just look at the next small "bite" on your "to-do list."

Organization

Any task is harder when you are disorganized. If you are having trouble getting your work done, try some of these approaches.

Clear off your desk surface. A cluttered, disordered work space can be much harder to work in, whereas a clean, neat desk top can help you feel calmer and more focused.

Gather all of the materials you will need. Make a list, then . get all your supplies together so you won't have to keep stopping or be tempted to socialize as you wander down the hall to borrow a stapler or computer paper.

Make a task list. Often students just jump into a task with no advance planning. This can lead to confusion and inefficiency, so always make lists of what you need to do.

Resisting Temptations

College is full of temptations. On many college campuses there is active "partying" four or more nights a week. In addition, there are the constant daily temptations to join the conversation down the hall or to go out for a pizza with your roommate.

Resist temptations through your choice of school. If it is hard for you to avoid temptations, you may want to select a school with a less social atmosphere.

If socializing instead of studying is a temptation, choose friends who are motivated and who study before they "party." If you are tempted to socialize when you study where you live, go to the library or to a removed study area.

If going to sleep is a temptation, don't study in or near your bed.

If staying up late is a temptation, set a "reverse alarm clock" —an alarm that reminds you to get ready to go to sleep. Many students with ADD or LD tend to get caught up in the activity of the moment and can easily lose track of time.

If you are tempted to skip classes, ask yourself why. Is it because it is an early morning class? Should you avoid signing up for 8:00 or 9:00 classes? Is it because the class meets on Friday afternoons and you are always tempted to leave early for the weekend? Are you skipping class because you are ill prepared? Bored? Rather than simply making a resolution to quit skipping class, you should try to understand what is going on in order to find the best solution for you.

Minimizing Distractions

Distractibility is often a problem for ADD/LD students. Dorm life can be especially distracting. The noise level in

many dorms is high and often goes on into the early morning hours. Discuss your distractibility with the Disabled Student Services office when you are applying to each school.

Some schools have "quiet dorms."

You may want to sign up for a single dorm room so that you are not distracted by a roommate.

As an upper classman you may want to live off-campus in a quieter environment.

If you have no choice but to live in a noisy dorm environment, you will need to find a quiet study place. If you cannot find one, discuss the problems with the DSS office.

Headphones can be helpful if you play quiet, calming music to screen out other distracting noises.

Reducing Frustrations

Many students with ADD or LD struggle with "low frustration tolerance." You may easily find yourself feeling so frustrated that you tend to give up a difficult task. As your frustration level rises, your ability to solve problems may decrease.

If you become so frustrated with a task that you cannot continue, get away from the task temporarily. Then get assistance in understanding and resolving your problem.

You may want to discuss your frustration with a tutor or counselor. Ask yourself the following questions:

- Do I understand the task? Am I frustrated because I need a tutor or some structured assistance?

- Would it be better to study with another student in the class?

- Do I need moral support? Would I feel better if I talked to other students in the class about how they are approaching the assignment?

- Should I work on this course in smaller "bites" because it is so difficult for me?

- Is this course too hard for me? Have I made a poor selection or received poor course advising in choosing the course?

- Should I drop the course?

Don't jump to this last conclusion first. Many students with ADD or LD drop courses they could have completed successfully if they had some help in working through the reasons for their frustration.

Building a Support Network

Many students enter college with anxiety about whether they will be able to succeed. Often they are away from home for the first time. They are suddenly in an environment where many decisions are left up to them. Reading and writing assignments can seem overwhelming. If you share some of these feelings, here are some ways to build confidence.

Look for as many supports as you can find on campus.

If there is an ADD/LD support group, join it. If there isn't, suggest to the DDS office that you would like to have one and encourage them or the counseling center to form one.

Be in frequent contact with your advisor. In the beginning you may want to visit your advisor several times a week for advice and moral support.

Don't wait until you are "in over your head." If you are not confident about your abilities in a course you are taking, get yourself a tutor at the beginning of the term.

Let your professors know of your learning problems and needs from the very beginning. Don't wait until you are having trouble in the class.

Learning Self-Advocacy

Join or help to form an ADD/LD student support group. You may need to find an active faculty sponsor for the group to continue successfully. Such a group will not only offer good emotional support, but can become a source of information regarding courses, professors, and study tips.

Read and talk about your areas of disability with your tutor or academic advisor until you are able to comfortably explain them. Many students with ADD/LD have been evaluated repeatedly, and yet are unable to fully explain their learning problems. You won't be successful in advocating for yourself until you are able to describe clearly the types of learning difficulties you have.

Approach each professor *at the beginning* of each course to explain your disability, how it may affect your performance in that particular class, and what accommodations or assistance you will need. Make an appointment to talk with each professor in his or her office. If you just grab a minute after class, you won't have the professor's full attention and you won't be as effective.

With the help of your advisor or tutor, write a one-page, jargon-free explanation of your learning problems and the accommodations you will need from your professor. You can make this more official by having the paper signed by both you and by the DSS office. Most of your professors probably know very little about learning disabilities. Even if they had time to read your complete record they wouldn't have the background to understand it. By explaining your needs succinctly, in language both you and the professor can easily understand, you will be a much more effective advocate for yourself. Having such a written statement is particularly important for students whose disability entails difficulty with verbal expression!

If you are having trouble in a particular class contact your professor on a regular basis for help and feedback. This lets the professor know that you are involved and making a full effort.

Be creative. If you have great difficulty with a certain type of assignment, suggest an alternative type of assignment to your professor. Just be sure that you are suggesting something that requires comparable time and effort.

Encourage your DSS office to form a student panel to educate the faculty regarding the needs of students with ADD/LD.

Don't hide your learning or attention problems from friends and faculty. Hiding it helps continue the misconception that ADD or LD means "dumb."

Extracurricular Activities

The opportunity to participate in extracurricular activities is an important aspect of your college experience. Making friends, building leadership and social skills, developing your athletic ability, and increasing your self-confidence are some of the many reasons why extracurricular activities can be important. Making smart choices of extracurricular involvement goes hand in hand with good time management.

It is easy to become overcommitted in college. If you choose to join a sorority or fraternity, the time commitment will be large. Participation in team athletics, likewise, requires a big time commitment.

Use time management techniques as you go through the process of committing to outside activities. Using your day planner, block out time that is already committed: class time, study time, meals, sleep, and relaxation.

Blocking out time for relaxation is important! You will need it, and you will take it whether it is scheduled or not. Unfortunately, "down time," or time to relax, often comes at the expense of study time if you have overcommitted yourself in other areas.

As you block out study time, be realistic. Students with ADD and LD usually are not able to work as efficiently as

49

other students. You will need more frequent study breaks in order to maintain concentration and focus.

Once you have blocked out your committed time, carefully assess whether you have time for the club, sport, or social activity you are considering. If you decide to play a sport that requires both afternoon practices and weekend games, you may have to decide to cut back on your weekend social life. Is this a trade-off you want to make? If your realistic answer is "yes," then go ahead with that commitment.

Some students with ADD/LD find that they function best when they are busy and when their days are structured. Such students may find that they waste more time and procrastinate more when they have large blocks of "free" time. Other students feel too stressed if most of their time is structured and committed. It may take you a couple of semesters to learn what your best patterns are.

Part-Time Employment

Many students need to work in order to pay for all or part of their college expenses. You should to be realistic about your energy level, organization level, and study requirements when making a work commitment. We strongly recommend that students with ADD and LD take a reduced course load of 12 hours per semester. If finances require you to work, you may need to reduce your course load to 9 hours. In many schools, 12 hours constitutes a full-time course load, but a student is classified as part-time if he or she takes fewer hours. You will need to discuss this requirement with the schools you are considering. In many schools, full-time student status is required to participate in certain activities on campus or to live on campus.

If money is your concern, you may want to investigate other ways to reduce your expenses. Students who are mature and who have good social skills may want to consider becoming a Resident Advisor in a dormitory. Often free housing is offered to RA's in exchange for functioning as a counselor and advisor for underclassmen.

Generally, on-campus jobs are preferable to off-campus jobs, even though they may pay less. Working on campus will help you feel integrated into the college community and will offer you another way to make friends. Supervisors of student employees working on campus will be more understanding if you need to take time off to write a paper or to study for finals. An off-campus employer, however, has a business to run, and may be far from supportive if you need time off.

Conclusion

We have discussed how to be a savvy consumer as you look for a college that can meet your needs. We have outlined services that, ideally, will be provided by the school that you attend. Because not all services are available on campus, we also have discussed the possibility of seeking some services in the professional community off campus. The most critical section of this book, however, is the last section, focusing on strategies for you to learn and to use. Not all of these approaches will work for you, but if you choose the tips that are appropriate for you and put them into action, you will be on the road to success in college. Choosing the right school is important, but it is even more essential for you to be educated about your learning and attention problems, and to take responsibility for managing them. We hope this book helps prepare you to take charge of your college experience.

We'd like to hear from you. If you have any ideas that we haven't thought to include in this manual, drop us a line and we may include your tips in our next edition. You can write to:

Kathleen G. Nadeau, Ph.D.
c/o Magination Press
19 Union Square West
New York, NY 10003

Resource List

◆ **Organizations:**

CH.A.D.D.
(Children and Adults with Attention Deficit Disorder)
499 NW 70th Avenue, Suite 308
Plantation, FL 33317
(305) 587-3700

LDA (Learning Disability Association)
4156 Library Road
Pittsburgh, PA 15234
(412) 341-1515

AHEAD
(Association on Higher Education and Disability)
P.O. Box 21192
Columbus, OH 43221-0192
(614) 488-4972

HEATH Resource Center
(National Clearinghouse on Postsecondary
Education for Individuals with Disabilities)
One Dupont Circle, Suite 800
Washington, DC 20036-1193
(800) 544-3284

◆ **Books:**

ADD and the College Student, edited by Patricia
Quinn. New York: Brunner/Mazel, 1994.

*Promoting Postsecondary Education for Students with
Learning Disabilities*, by Loring Brinckerhoff, Stan
Shaw & Joan McGuire. Austin, TX: Pro-Ed, 1993.

*Success for College Students with Learning Disabili-
ties*, edited by Susan Vogel & Pamela Adelman. New
York: Springer-Verlag, 1993.

◆ Directories:

The K&W Guide to Colleges for the Learning Disabled, edited by Marybeth Kravets & Imy F. Wax. New York: HarperCollins, 1992.

Peterson's Guide to Colleges with Programs for Students with Learning Disabilities, edited by Charles T. Mangrum, III & Stephen S. Strichart. Princeton, NJ: Petersons Guides, 1992.

Unlocking Potential: College and Other Choices for Learning Disabled People: A Step-by-Step Guide, by Barbara Scheiber & Jeane Talpers. Chevy Chase, MD: Adler & Adler, 1987.

About the Author

Kathleen Nadeau, Ph.D., is a clinical psychologist who specializes in working with adolescents and adults who have learning and attentional problems. As the parent of a college student who has both ADD and LD issues to cope with, the tips and strategies in this book take on a special meaning for her. She has seen many students go from academic failure and despair to academic success, graduation, and even on to graduate school by using the tools outlined in this book. Dr. Nadeau is the co-author of *Learning to Slow Down and Pay Attention,* a book for elementary school children with ADD. She is a contributor to the book *ADD and the College Student,* edited by Patricia Quinn, M.D. Dr. Nadeau is the director of Chesapeake Psychological Services of Maryland, a private clinic that specializes in diagnosing and treating people of all ages who have learning and attentional difficulties.

About the Photographer

Sylvia Johnson is a freelance photographer who has worked in the Washington, DC area for over 20 years. She has recently recognized that she has had to cope with learning and attentional problems throughout her life, and hopes through her participation in this project to increase the awareness of these issues. She hopes that students today will receive the assistance that was not available to her.